THE INDIAN SILK ROAD

A HISTORICAL AND CULTURAL EXPLORATION OF THE TRADE ROUTES THAT CONNECTED INDIA TO THE WORLD

DR. JAGADEESH PILLAI

|| *"Dedicated to all who seek to understand and appreciate Indian culture and tradition."* ||

Contents

Contents

Pryaer

"Om Sahanaa Vavatu Sahanau Bhunaktu Saha Veeryam
Karavaavahai Tejasvi Naavadheetamastu Maa
Vidvishaavahai Om Shantih Shantih Shantih"

The literal interpretation of this mantra is: OM. Let us all
protect one another, let us all share in joy, let us all work
together and let our learning be illuminated. Let us be
united in peace,
OM Peace, Peace, Peace.

About The Author

Dr. Jagadeesh Pillai is a renowned Guinness World Record holder, writer, and researcher hailing from Varanasi, also known as the abode of Lord Shiva. With a Ph.D. in Vedic Science and a range of creative ideas and achievements, he is a true polymath. He is the author of more than 100 books including Research Publications. Although his roots can be traced back to Kerala, the people of Varanasi hold him in high regard and affectionately consider him one of their own.

Dr. Pillai has achieved four Guinness World Records in the following subjects:

"Script to Screen" - In this record, Dr. Pillai produced and directed an animation film within the shortest time possible, breaking the previous record set by Canadians. He has also received numerous national and international awards and recognitions for this achievement.

Longest Line of Postcards - For this record, Dr. Pillai created a line of 16,300 postcards on the occasion of the 163rd anniversary of Indian Postal Day. The event also included a questionnaire about the Indian flag.

Largest Poster Awareness Campaign - Dr. Pillai designed an awareness campaign on the subject of "Beti Bachao - Beti Padhao" (Save the Girl Child - Educate the Girl Child) to achieve this record.

Largest Envelope - In tribute to the Indian Prime Minister's

"Make in India" initiative, Dr. Pillai created a 4000 square meter envelope using waste paper to achieve this record.

Attempted - **70000 Candles on a 210 kg Cake** - To celebrate the 70th Indian Independence Day, Dr. Pillai attempted to light 70,000 candles on a 210 kg cake, which was recorded in World Records India.

Attempted - **Documentary on Dhamek Stupa of Sarnath in 17 Languages** - Dr. Pillai attempted to create a documentary on the Dhamek Stupa of Sarnath, dubbing it in 17 different languages. The result of this attempt is currently awaiting confirmation from the Guinness World Records.

Dr. Pillai is skilled in teaching the Bhagavad Gita, a Hindu scripture, and is popular among young people. He has helped many young people improve their lives through his motivational teachings.

In addition to teaching, he has composed and sung numerous Sanskrit Bhajans and patriotic songs.

He has also written and directed several short films and documentaries for awareness campaigns, and has volunteered with the police in both UP and Kerala to spread awareness about various issues through videos and photography.

Incredibly, he has produced and directed over 100 documentaries about the city of Varanasi, all on his own.

He has also helped and guided more than 25 boys and girls to achieve world records through creative and innovative methods. He is a multifaceted person who uses his intellect and the blessings given to him by God to excel in various areas. He is both a teacher and a student, always learning and teaching, and is able to master any subject he comes across.

He is a selfless social activist and motivational speaker who has overcome struggles and failures to become a successful and enthusiastic individual with a rich life experience.

In addition to his work with the Bhagavad Gita, he is also an efficient Tarot card reader, Astro-Vastu consultant, and a talented singer and composer. He has sung the entire Ram Charita Manas and Bhagavad Gita in his own compositions, and has sung the phrase "Lokah Samastha Sukhino Bhavantu" in 50 different languages. He is currently working on a detailed and scientific study of Vedas, Upanishads, Puranas, and the Bhagavad Gita. He has also composed and sung the Hanuman Chalisa and Gayatri Mantra in 108 and 1008 different compositions, respectively.

Awards - Four Times Guinness World Records, Winner of Mahatma Gandhi Vishwa Shanti Puraskar, Mahatma Gandhi Global Peace Ambassador, Kashi Ratna Award, Dr. APJ Abdul Kalam Motivational Person of the Year 2017, Mother Teresa Award, Indira Gandhi Priyadarshini Award, Bharat Vikas Ratna Award, Udyog Ratna Award, Vigyan Prasar Award, Poorvanchal Ratn Samman.

Preface

The Indian Silk Road: A Historical And Cultural Exploration Of The Trade Routes That Connected India To The World is a comprehensive exploration of one of the most important trade routes in history. Spanning from ancient times to the present, this book delves into the economic, cultural, and religious significance of the Indian Silk Road and its impact on the world.

The Indian Silk Road, also known as the Silk Route, connected India to the neighboring regions, including Central Asia, China, and Europe. The trade along the Indian Silk Road has increased significantly in recent years, with an emphasis on the exchange of goods and services, including textiles, agricultural products, and natural resources. The Indian Silk Road also played a crucial role in the spread of Buddhism, Zoroastrianism and other religions and cultures, and their exchange and mutual influence.

This book is divided into 15 chapters, which cover a wide range of topics related to the Indian Silk Road. The chapters explore the origins of the Indian Silk Road, the development of trade networks, the role of the Indian Silk Road in the spread of Buddhism, Zoroastrianism and other religions, the influence of the British East India Company, and the modern era of the Indian Silk Road.

The book is intended for a general audience, including scholars, students, and anyone interested in the history and culture of the Indian Silk Road. It provides a detailed and comprehensive account of one of the most important trade routes in history and its lasting impact on the world.

The Indian Silk Road: A Historical And Cultural Exploration Of The Trade Routes That Connected India To The World is an important contribution to our understanding of the past, present, and future of the Indian Silk Road, and will be a valuable resource for anyone interested in the history and culture of the Indian Silk Road.

I

Introduction: The Indian Silk Road and Its Significance

The Indian Silk Road, also known as the Spice Route, was a network of trade routes that connected India to the rest of the world for over 2,000 years. These routes facilitated the exchange of goods, culture, religion, and ideas between the East and West, and played a crucial role in shaping the history and development of the Indian subcontinent

The Indian Silk Road was one of the most important trade routes in the ancient world, connecting India to the Mediterranean, Central Asia, and China. The routes were used to trade a wide variety of goods, including spices, textiles, precious stones, and metals. The most valuable and sought-after goods, however, were silk and spices, which gave the routes their name.

The Indian Silk Road was not just a trade route, but also a cultural and religious exchange. The routes facilitated the spread of Buddhism, which emerged in India in the 6th century BC and spread to China and Central Asia through the Silk Road. The routes also played a role in the spread of other religions such as Islam and Christianity.

The Indian Silk Road also played a significant role in the spread of science and technology. Indian scholars, scientists and craftsmen traveled along the routes and shared their knowledge with their counterparts in Central Asia and China. This led to the exchange of ideas and the development of new technologies such as papermaking, gunpowder, and the compass.

The Indian Silk Road had a profound impact on the history and development of the Indian subcontinent. It shaped the economy, culture, and society of the region and continues to be an important part of India's heritage today. The Indian Silk Road is a fascinating subject that provides a glimpse into the past and helps us understand the interconnectedness of the world.

The Indian Silk Road was a network of trade routes that connected India to the rest of the world for over 2,000 years. It played a crucial role in shaping the history and development of the Indian subcontinent by facilitating the exchange of goods, culture, religion, and ideas between the East and West. The Indian Silk Road is an important part of India's heritage and continues to be a fascinating subject for historians, archaeologists, and anyone interested in the past.

"The Indian textile is not merely a piece of cloth, but a work of art that tells a story."
- Ritu Kumar

౷

II

Ancient Trade Routes: The Origins of the Indian Silk Road

The Indian Silk Road, also known as the Spice Route, was a network of trade routes that connected India to the rest of the world for over 2,000 years. These routes facilitated the exchange of goods, culture, religion, and ideas between the East and West, and played a crucial role in shaping the history and development of the Indian subcontinent.

The origins of the Indian Silk Road can be traced back to the Indus Valley Civilization, which emerged in the region around 2600 BCE. This civilization was known for its advanced urban planning and sophisticated trade networks, which included long-distance trade routes that connected the Indus Valley to the neighboring regions. The

Indus Valley Civilization traded a wide variety of goods, including precious stones, metals, and textiles, which laid the foundations for the Indian Silk Road.

The Indian Silk Road as we know it today, began to take shape in the 4th century BCE during the time of the Mauryan Empire. The Mauryan Empire controlled a large part of the Indian subcontinent and established a network of trade routes that connected India to the neighboring regions. The Mauryans traded a wide variety of goods, including spices, textiles, and precious stones, which were in high demand in the neighboring regions.

During the Gupta Empire (320-550 CE) the Indian Silk Road reached its golden age. The Gupta Empire controlled a large part of the Indian subcontinent and established a network of trade routes that connected India to Central Asia and China. The Guptas traded a wide variety of goods, including silk, spices, and precious stones, which were in high demand in the neighboring regions. This period is considered as the peak of the Indian Silk Road as it was a time of prosperity and cultural flourishing.

The origins of the Indian Silk Road can be traced back to the Indus Valley Civilization, which emerged in the region around 2600 BCE. The Indian Silk Road as we know it today, began to take shape in the 4th century BCE during the time of the Mauryan Empire, and reached its golden age during the Gupta Empire (320-550 CE) . These ancient trade routes played a crucial role in shaping the history and development of the Indian subcontinent by facilitating the exchange of goods, culture, religion, and ideas between the East and West.

*"Textile is the thread that runs through the
tapestry of Indian culture."*
- Manish Arora

౲

III

The Mauryan Empire and the Development of Trade Networks

The Mauryan Empire was one of the largest and most powerful empires in the ancient world, with its capital in Pataliputra, present-day Patna, Bihar. The empire controlled a large part of the Indian subcontinent, and its rulers were known for their administrative and military prowess. One of the key achievements of the Mauryan Empire was the development of trade networks and the expansion of trade across the Indian subcontinent.

During the reign of the Mauryan Empire, trade routes were established that connected India to the neighboring regions, including Central Asia and China. These trade routes facilitated the exchange of goods, culture, religion, and ideas between the East and West, and played a crucial role in shaping the history and development of the Indian subcontinent. The Mauryans traded a wide variety of goods, including spices, textiles, and precious stones, which were in high demand in the neighboring regions.

The Mauryan Empire also developed an efficient system of administration and taxation, which helped to facilitate trade and commerce. The empire had a vast network of roads and rest houses, which made travel and transportation of goods easier. The empire also had a system of standardized weights and measures, which helped to regulate trade and prevent fraud.

The Mauryan Empire played a crucial role in the development of trade networks in ancient India, specifically in the context of the Indian Silk Road. The empire established trade routes that connected India to the neighboring regions, including Central Asia and China, which facilitated the exchange of goods, culture, religion, and ideas between the East and West. The Mauryan Empire also developed an efficient system of administration and taxation, which helped to facilitate trade and commerce, and supported the expansion of the Indian Silk Road.

"Indian textiles are a unique blend of tradition and modernity, reflecting the country's rich cultural heritage."
- Sabyasachi Mukherjee

IV

The Gupta Empire and the Golden Age of Indian Trade

The Gupta Empire was a powerful empire in ancient India, which controlled a large part of the Indian subcontinent from around 320 CE to 550 CE. The empire was known for its prosperity, cultural achievements, and advancements in science and technology. One of the key achievements of the Gupta Empire was the expansion of trade and commerce across the Indian subcontinent.

During the reign of the Gupta Empire, trade routes were established and expanded that connected India to the neighboring regions, including Central Asia and China. These trade routes facilitated the exchange of goods, culture, religion, and ideas between the East and West, and played a crucial role in shaping the history and development of the Indian subcontinent. The Gupta Empire traded a wide variety of goods, including silk, spices, and precious stones, which were in high demand in the neighboring regions.

The Gupta Empire also played a crucial role in the development of the Indian Silk Road as it reached its golden age during this period. The empire controlled a large part of the Indian subcontinent and established a network of trade routes that connected India to Central Asia and China. The Guptas traded a wide variety of goods, including silk, spices, and precious stones, which were in high demand in the neighboring regions. This period was a time of prosperity and cultural flourishing, and it is considered as the peak of the Indian Silk Road.

The Gupta Empire played a crucial role in the development of trade in ancient India, specifically in the context of the Indian Silk Road. The empire established and expanded trade routes that connected India to the neighboring regions, including Central Asia and China, which facilitated the exchange of goods, culture, religion, and ideas between the East and West. The Gupta Empire also played a crucial role in the development of the Indian Silk Road as it reached its golden age during this period.

"Indian textiles are a symbol of our rich culture, our heritage, and our identity as a nation."
- Manish Malhotra

V

Religious and Cultural Exchange Along the Indian Silk Road

The Indian Silk Road was not just a trade route, but also a cultural and religious exchange. The routes facilitated the spread of Buddhism, which emerged in India in the 6th century BCE and spread to China and Central Asia through the Silk Road. Buddhist monks, scholars and merchants traveled along the routes and spread the teachings of Buddha, and also translated texts into different languages for the benefit of local people. This led to the establishment of Buddhist monasteries and temples along the routes and the spread of Buddhism throughout Central Asia and China.

The Indian Silk Road also played a role in the spread of other religions such as Islam and Christianity. Arab traders and merchants, who traveled along the Silk Road, brought Islam to India and it was adopted by some of the local population. Similarly, Christian missionaries, who traveled along the Silk Road, brought Christianity to India and it was adopted by some of the local population.

The Indian Silk Road also facilitated the exchange of culture and ideas between the East and West. Indian merchants, scholars and artists traveled along the routes and shared their culture and ideas with their counterparts in Central Asia and China. This led to the exchange of ideas and the development of new technologies such as papermaking, gunpowder, and the compass.

The Indian Silk Road was not just a trade route, but also a cultural and religious exchange. The routes facilitated the spread of Buddhism, Islam, and Christianity, and also the exchange of culture and ideas between the East and West. This exchange of religion and culture played a crucial role in shaping the history and development of the Indian subcontinent and the neighboring regions.

"Indian textiles are a unique blend of tradition and modernity, reflecting the country's rich cultural heritage."
- Sabyasachi Mukherjee

VI

The Rajput Kingdoms and the Indian Silk Road

The Rajputs were a Hindu warrior caste that emerged in the northwestern region of India around the 8th century CE. They established several powerful kingdoms in the region, including Mewar, Marwar, and Mewat, which controlled a significant portion of the Indian subcontinent. The Rajput kingdoms played a crucial role in the Indian Silk Road as they controlled key trade routes that connected India to the neighboring regions, including Central Asia and China.

The Rajput kingdoms were known for their wealth and prosperity, and they played a significant role in the Indian economy. They traded a wide variety of goods, including textiles, spices, and precious stones, which were in high demand in the neighboring regions. The Rajputs also controlled the production and trade of luxury goods, such as silk, which was a highly sought-after commodity along the Indian Silk Road.

The Rajput kingdoms also played a significant role in the cultural and religious exchange along the Indian Silk Road. They were patrons of art and architecture, and they built grand temples and palaces that reflect their rich culture and heritage. They also patronized scholars, poets, and artists, which led to the development of a rich literary and cultural tradition in the region.

The Rajput kingdoms played a crucial role in the Indian Silk Road as they controlled key trade routes that connected India to the neighboring regions, including Central Asia and China. They were known for their wealth and prosperity, and they played a significant role in the Indian economy. They also played a significant role in the cultural and religious exchange along the Indian Silk Road. The Rajputs were patrons of art and architecture, and they built grand temples and palaces that reflect their rich culture and heritage.

"The beauty of Indian textiles lies in the intricate designs and the rich colors that tell the story of our culture."
- Neeru Kumar

VII

The Mughal Empire and the Expansion of Indian Trade

The Mughal Empire was a powerful empire in India that emerged in the 16th century and controlled a large part of the Indian subcontinent until the 18th century. The Mughals were known for their military prowess, administrative skills, and cultural achievements. One of their key achievements was the expansion of trade and commerce in India, particularly along the Indian Silk Road.

During the reign of the Mughal Empire, trade routes were expanded and new ones were created that connected India to the neighboring regions, including Central Asia, China, and Europe. These trade routes facilitated the exchange of goods, culture, religion, and ideas between the East and

West, and played a crucial role in shaping the history and development of the Indian subcontinent. The Mughals traded a wide variety of goods, including textiles, spices, and precious stones, which were in high demand in the neighboring regions. They also controlled the production and trade of luxury goods, such as silk, which was a highly sought-after commodity along the Indian Silk Road.

The Mughals also played a significant role in the cultural and religious exchange along the Indian Silk Road. They were patrons of art and architecture, and they built grand temples, palaces, and monuments that reflect their rich culture and heritage. They also patronized scholars, poets, and artists, which led to the development of a rich literary and cultural tradition in the region.

The Mughal Empire played a crucial role in the expansion of trade in India, specifically in the context of the Indian Silk Road. The Mughals expanded and created new trade routes that connected India to the neighboring regions, including Central Asia, China, and Europe.

These trade routes facilitated the exchange of goods, culture, religion, and ideas between the East and West, and played a crucial role in shaping the history and development of the Indian subcontinent. The Mughals also played a significant role in the cultural and religious exchange along the Indian Silk Road, and were patrons of art and architecture, and they built grand temples, palaces, and monuments that reflect their rich culture and heritage.

৩

"Indian textiles are not just a fashion statement, but a celebration of our ancient traditions and culture."
- Rohit Bal

☙

VIII

The British East India Company and the Impact on Indian Trade

The British East India Company was a powerful trading company that was established in 1600 and was granted a monopoly on trade with the East Indies by the British government. The company played a significant role in the Indian trade, particularly in the context of the Indian Silk Road.

The company had a significant impact on Indian trade as it controlled a large part of the Indian economy, especially in the areas of textiles, spices, and precious stones. They also controlled the trade of luxury goods such as silk, which was a highly sought-after commodity along the Indian Silk Road. The company also controlled the trade of opium, which was grown in India and sold to China, which caused a significant impact on the Indian economy.

The British East India Company also played a significant role in the cultural and religious exchange along the Indian Silk Road. The company patronized scholars, poets, and artists, which led to the development of a rich literary and cultural tradition in the region. However, the company also had a negative impact on the Indian culture and tradition as it introduced British customs and beliefs, which caused a significant change in the Indian society.

The British East India Company played a significant role in the Indian trade, specifically in the context of the Indian Silk Road. The company controlled a large part of the Indian economy and had a significant impact on Indian trade, particularly in the areas of textiles, spices, and precious stones. The British East India Company also played a significant role in the cultural and religious exchange along the Indian Silk Road, but it also had a negative impact on the Indian culture and tradition as it introduced British customs and beliefs, which caused a significant change in the Indian society.

"Indian textiles are an integral part of our
heritage, reflecting the diversity and richness
of our culture."
- Anamika Khanna

IX

The Silk Road and the Spread of Buddhism

Buddhism spread from India to other parts of Asia, including Central Asia and China, through the Silk Road. Buddhist monks, scholars, and merchants traveled along the routes and spread the teachings of Buddha. They also translated texts into different languages for the benefit of local people. This led to the establishment of Buddhist monasteries and temples along the routes and the spread of Buddhism throughout Central Asia and China.

The Silk Road also facilitated the spread of Buddhism by promoting cultural and religious exchange. Indian merchants, scholars, and artists traveled along the routes and shared their culture and ideas with their counterparts in Central Asia and China. This led to the exchange of ideas and the development of new technologies such as papermaking, gunpowder, and the compass.

The Silk Road also played a role in the development of different schools of Buddhism. As the teachings of Buddha spread along the Silk Road, different interpretations and practices of Buddhism developed in different regions, leading to the emergence of different schools of Buddhism such as Theravada, Mahayana and Vajrayana.

The Silk Road played a crucial role in the spread of Buddhism. Buddhist monks, scholars, and merchants traveled along the routes and spread the teachings of Buddha, which led to the establishment of Buddhist monasteries and temples along the routes and the spread of Buddhism throughout Central Asia and China. The Silk Road also facilitated the spread of Buddhism by promoting cultural and religious exchange, and also played a role in the development of different schools of Buddhism.

"Indian textiles are a reflection of our rich history, our vibrant culture, and our deep-rooted traditions."
- Narendra Kumar

X

The Silk Road and the Transmission of Science and Technology

The Silk Road played a crucial role in the transmission of science and technology between the East and West. The trade routes facilitated the exchange of ideas, goods, and technologies between different cultures and civilizations. This led to the spread of new technologies and scientific knowledge, which had a significant impact on the economic, social and cultural development of the regions connected by the Silk Road.

One of the most important technological innovations transmitted along the Silk Road was the invention of paper. Paper was first invented in China around 105 CE and it quickly spread along the Silk Road to other parts of Asia, including India, Central Asia, and the Middle East. Paper revolutionized the way people communicated and recorded information, which led to the development of written literature, education and the spread of knowledge.

The Silk Road also played a crucial role in the transmission of scientific knowledge and mathematical concepts. Indian scholars and merchants traveled along the routes and shared their knowledge of mathematics, astronomy, and medicine with their counterparts in Central Asia and China. This led to the development of new technologies and advancements in these fields.

The Silk Road played a crucial role in the transmission of science and technology between the East and West. The trade routes facilitated the exchange of ideas, goods, and technologies between different cultures and civilizations, which led to the spread of new technologies and scientific knowledge.

This had a significant impact on the economic, social, and cultural development of the regions connected by the Silk Road, and it helped to create an interconnected network of cultures and civilizations, with a shared knowledge and understanding of science and technology.

XI

The Indian Silk Road and the Spread of Zoroastrianism

Zoroastrianism, also known as Mazdayasna, is an ancient religion founded by the prophet Zoroaster in ancient Iran. The religion spread throughout the Iranian plateau and beyond, including Central Asia and India, through the Silk Road trade routes. Zoroastrian merchants and scholars traveled along the routes and spread the teachings of Zoroaster to the people they encountered. This led to the establishment of Zoroastrian communities along the Silk Road and the spread of Zoroastrianism throughout the region.

The Silk Road also facilitated the spread of Zoroastrianism by promoting cultural and religious exchange. Zoroastrian merchants, scholars, and artists traveled along the routes and shared their culture and ideas with their counterparts in Central Asia and India. This led to the exchange of ideas and the development of new technologies, such as papermaking, gunpowder, and the compass.

The Silk Road also played a role in the development of different schools of Zoroastrianism. As the teachings of Zoroaster spread along the Silk Road, different interpretations and practices of Zoroastrianism developed in different regions, leading to the emergence of different schools of Zoroastrianism such as the Parsi Zoroastrianism which is found in India.

The Indian Silk Road played a crucial role in the spread of Zoroastrianism. Zoroastrian merchants and scholars traveled along the routes and spread the teachings of Zoroaster, which led to the establishment of Zoroastrian communities along the Silk Road and the spread of Zoroastrianism throughout the region. The Silk Road also facilitated the spread of Zoroastrianism by promoting cultural and religious exchange and played a role in the development of different schools of Zoroastrianism.

XII

The Indian Silk Road in the Modern Era

The Indian Silk Road, also known as the Silk Route, has played a vital role in the economic and cultural development of the regions it connected. In the modern era, the Indian Silk Road has taken on new significance as an important trade route that connects India to the neighboring regions, including Central Asia, China, and Europe. The trade along the Indian Silk Road has increased significantly in recent years, with an emphasis on the exchange of goods and services, including textiles, agricultural products, and natural resources.

The Indian Silk Road also plays a significant role in the cultural and religious exchange between the East and West. The route has been a conduit for the spread of ideas, customs, and traditions, which has led to a greater understanding and appreciation of different cultures.

In recent years, there has been renewed interest in the Indian Silk Road as a potential economic corridor that could connect India to Central Asia and Europe. This is driven by the increasing demand for natural resources, such as oil and gas, and the potential for greater trade and economic cooperation between the regions.

The Indian Silk Road in the Modern Era plays an important role in the economic, cultural, and political context, connecting India to the neighboring regions, including Central Asia, China, and Europe. The trade along the Indian Silk Road has increased significantly in recent years, with an emphasis on the exchange of goods and services, including textiles, agricultural products, and natural resources.

The Indian Silk Road also plays a significant role in the cultural and religious exchange between the East and West and the renewed interest in the Indian Silk Road as a potential economic corridor that could connect India to Central Asia and Europe.

XIII

The Legacy of the Indian Silk Road

The Indian Silk Road, also known as the Silk Route, has played a crucial role in the economic, cultural, and religious development of the regions it connected. The trade routes facilitated the exchange of goods, ideas, and technologies between different cultures and civilizations, which led to the spread of new technologies and scientific knowledge. This had a significant impact on the economic, social, and cultural development of the regions connected by the Silk Road, and it helped to create an interconnected network of cultures and civilizations, with a shared knowledge and understanding of science and technology.

The Indian Silk Road also played a crucial role in the spread of Buddhism, Zoroastrianism and other religions and cultures, and their exchange and mutual influence. The Silk Road also played a significant role in the development of different schools of Buddhism, Zoroastrianism, and other religions.

The Indian Silk Road has left a lasting legacy in the form of the cultural and architectural heritage of the regions it connected. The route has been a conduit for the spread of ideas, customs, and traditions, which has led to a greater understanding and appreciation of different cultures.

In the modern era, the Indian Silk Road continues to play an important role in the economic, cultural, and political context. The renewed interest in the Indian Silk Road as a potential economic corridor that could connect India to Central Asia and Europe, and the trade along the Indian Silk Road has increased significantly in recent years, with an emphasis on the exchange of goods and services, including textiles, agricultural products, and natural resources.

The Indian Silk Road has played a crucial role in the economic, cultural, and religious development of the regions it connected. The trade routes facilitated the exchange of goods, ideas, and technologies between different cultures and civilizations, which led to the spread of new technologies and scientific knowledge.

The Indian Silk Road has left a lasting legacy in the form of the cultural and architectural heritage of the regions it connected and continues to play an important role in the modern era as well.

OTHER BOOKS OF THE AUTHOR

1. The Moments When I Met God
2. Kashiyile Theertha Pathangal
3. GURU GYAN VANI
4. Abhiprerak Gita
5. ASSI SE JAIN GHAT TAK
6. Hopelessness of Arjuna
7. The Soul and It's True Nature
8. Sense of Action (Karma)
9. Action through Wisdom
10. Action through Wisdom
11. THEORY AND PRACTICAL OF EVERY ACTION
12. LOGICAL UNDERSTANDING OF THE SUPREME
13. THE IMPERISHABLE SUPREME
14. Yatra Nishadraj se Hanuman Ghat Tak
15. Yatra Karnatak Ghat se Raja Ghat Tak
16. Yatra Pandey Ghat se Prayagraj Ghat Tak
17. Yatra Ranjendra Prasad Ghat se Dattatreya Ghat Tak
18. YaatraSindhiya Ghat se Gwaliar Ghat Tak
19. Yatra Mangala Gauri Ghat se Hanuman Gadhi Ghat Tak
20. Yatra Gaay Ghat Se Nishad Ghat Tak
21. MAA GANGA, GHATEN EVM UTSAV
22. Ganga Arti Dev Deepavali evam Any Utsav
23. Potentials of Digitalized India
24. VEDIC CONSCIOUSNESS
25. A Brief Introduction to Vedic Science
26. Kashi ke Barah Jyotirling
27. IMPACT OF MOTIVATION
28. Let's have a Milky Way Journey
29. Color Therapy in a Nutshell

30. Rigveda in a Nutshell
31. Yajurveda in a Nutshell
32. Samveda in a Nutshell
33. Atharva Veda in a Nutshell
34. Ayushman Bhava - Ayurveda
35. Srimad Bhagavad Gita and Upanishad Connection
36. Srimad Bhagavad Gita - an attempt to summarize each chapter.
37. Facts and Impact of Nakshatra
38. Astro Gems - NAVARATNA
39. Ekadashi - A Concise Overview
40. A Concise View of Hanuman Chalisa
41. Inspirational Gita
42. Nakshatraranyam
43. Summary of 18 Mahapuranas
44. Synopsis of 18 Upa Puranas
45. Rigvediya Upanishads
46. Shukla Yajurvediya Upanishads
47. Krishna Yajurvediya Upanishads
48. Samavediya Upanishads
49. Atharvavediya Upanishads
50. The Seven Great Sages
51. From Rocket Scientist to President Dr. APJ Abdul Kalam
52. The Visionary's Voice - Quotes of Dr. APJ Abdul Kalam
53. The Wisdom of Swami Vivekananda: Insights and Inspiration from a Legendary Spiritual Teacher
54. Ayurvedic Remedies from the Garden
55. Sages and Seers
56. Rising Strong – Motivational Stories of Women
57. Beyond Flames -Mystery stories of Funeral Ghat Manikarnika
58. The Origins of Tulsi: A Look at the Mythological Roots of the Plant"

ॐ

Contact

DR. JAGADEESH PILLAI

PhD in Vedic Science

Four Times Guinness World Record Holder

Winner of Mahatma Gandhi Vishwa Shanti Puraskar and
Global Peace Ambassador

Gemology, Astro & Vastu Consultant - Spiritual Counselor

Consultant for designing World Record Ideas

Efficient Tarot Card Reader

9839093003

myrichindia@gmail.com

drjagadeeshpillai@facebook

drjagadeeshpillai@instagram

jagadeeshpillai@youtube

www. JAGADEESHPILLAI.com

൏

|| LOKAHA SAMASTHAHA SUKHINO BHAVANTU ||

• 55 •